The Rainbow Series (
To Touch The Heart

C000019677

RAINBOW OF LIFE

love & light,
Chrissy Greenslade

Rainbow of Life   *Book One*

Poetry by Chrissy Greenslade.
Illustrations by Josephine Winzar.

PETRA PUBLISHING

RAINBOW OF LIFE

ISBN: 0 953431908

First Edition published Spring 1999 by
PETRA PUBLISHING
4, Leven Close
Bournemouth
BH4 9LP

> "*I dedicate this book,*
> *To all those whom I love*
> *In this world and the next,*
> *And to all those who need love.*"

British Library Cataloguing in Publication Data:
A catalogue record for this book is available from the British Library

Printed in China through World Print Ltd.

Layout & Design Mark A Fudge

CONTENTS

ACKNOWLEDGEMENTS

The following poems have previously been published in the following magazines and annuals.

The Friendship Book

Treasure
Right Thinking
Common Senses

Secrets

Crowning Glory
My Handyman
Preparation
Diet Dilemma

The Science of Thought Review

I thought I'd never love again
The Same Difference
Release
Spiritual Pathway
God's Protection
Unconditional Love
The Power of Love

My Weekly

Taken Down a Peg or Two
The Deerstalker Hat
My Perfect Day

The Christian Herald

Friendship

The Fireside Book

Weeds Welcome

Woman's Weekly

Love Recaptured

The People's Friend

Golden Memories
Who could ask for more?
The Dress Fitting
Bluebells

The Journal (DHWSHA)

Walk with Angels
Tomorrow never comes

The People's Friend Annual

To share is to care

INTRODUCTION

I've always wanted to reach the ordinary person who enjoys sincere, simple poetry, which comes direct from the heart. I knew the only way to do this, was to produce a book that was suitable as a 'Gift Book,'which was not overpriced.

I've been given the gift of writing and the only motive I have in writing this series, is not for profit but to share my gift, especially the love and hope my books contain.

One of the most pleasing comments was made by a friend, reading my poetry for the first time. "How nice to be able to read poetry that I can understand and enjoy straightaway!"

'Poetry is my life,' is a big statement, but it is certainly the biggest part of mine. Unless I have spent some time writing each day, my soul feels bereft.

My poems are about life in all its rainbow colours. They are based on my life and my reactions to life. I know many of you will identify with my situations. I only feel a poem 'coming on', when I am moved by love, laughter or emotion.

I know why God gave me the gift of writing poetry. It is to bring laughter, hope, comfort, faith and compassion into people's lives. If only one poem touches you or gives your life new meaning then in this first book I have succeeded.

In this series of books I hope to share with you my rainbow of life. Cross over the rainbow with me.

Love and Light, Chrissy.

For further information, book requirements, poetry readings and talks please contact
Petra Publishing, 4, Leven Close, Bournemouth, BH4 9LP   Tel: 01202 762730

MIRACLE OF SPRING

Snow blossom bursting in the hedge,
Today we felt the joy of spring,
Excited birds and bumble bees,
And hope itself was on the wing.

Martins saluted their return,
A lone first swallow took its rest,
Moorhens and coots, shrill seagulls called,
To busy rooks building their nest.

Lawn-cutting perfume filled the air,
And damp, fresh earth of after-showers,
A yellow Brimstone butterfly,
With fragile wings swayed on the flowers.

Bright daffodils and celandines,
Held up their heads to greet the morn,
The flowering cherries plumped their buds,
Star daisies sparkled on the lawn.

As hand in hand our senses reeled,
God's miracle made spirits soar,
With footsteps light, hearts filled with hope,
We smiled - for it was Spring once more.

CROWNING GLORY

I'm yawning and I'm dreaming,
As my locks are warmed and set,
I've read two women's magazines,
The latest I can get.

I've drunk a cup of coffee,
And I've visited the loo,
I've gazed at other customers,
With hairstyles neat and new.

I really need a manicure,
I am glad I wore new shoes,
I think I'll have a face pack soon,
Some treatment I could use.

I'll plan tomorrow's meal time,
To make it more inviting,
I've time to think of holidays,
Help life feel more exciting.

My ears are hot and glowing,
And my set is nearly dry,
Oh, help, those can't be rain
  clouds that
Are threatening the sky?

That's good the sun is winning,
So my style will stay alright,
How nice to take these rollers out,
And not look such a fright.

Now is the tension mounting,
As with skill Theresa's hand,
Brushes and combs and titivates
Into the 'Promised Land'.

This sophisticated creature,
Who on earth now can she be,
With upswept hair - though
  shiny nose,
Who's gazing back at me?

It really is amazing,
How she has transformed my head,
The only problem I can see,
Is how I'll sleep in bed!

I THOUGHT I'D NEVER LOVE AGAIN

I never thought I'd love again,
I thought that I would die,
I never thought I'd laugh again,
I tried so not to cry.

My strength it was incredible,
My faith it was unshaken,
I said I'd never want such love
In me to reawaken.

I wouldn't watch more suffering,
Or share more hurt or pain,
I felt that I should live alone,
And never love again.

But God had different plans for me,
I didn't stand a chance,
For I was linked with you my love,
That day, from our first glance.

So torn between my love for you,
And longing to be free,
I let my Spirits guide me on
This blessed destiny.

And now we are together, bathed
In happiness not pain,
My dearest I'm so very glad,
I've learned to love again.

TAKEN DOWN A PEG OR TWO

When I am very busy,
Or I'm feeling sick and ill,
My other half's so helpful,
Filled with kindness and goodwill.
He says, "I'll hang the clothes out,"
And he does his very best.
I grimace as I see the way,
That he's hung his shirt and vest.

Do other housewives just like me,
Suffer the same disease,
Stand gazing at their washing,
As it's blowing in the breeze,
And notice as they take the prop,
To push it way up high,
Tea cloths are hanging upside down,
As they gaily flutter by?

The flower is growing downwards,
And a gnome stands on his head,
The writing on the kitchen towel,
Can't possibly be read;
The panties are uneven
And my blouses are askew,
His sweater will have shoulder
   bumps,
Oh, he hasn't got a clue!

His socks are hung for Santa Claus,
Instead of by the toes,
Though why it matters I can't say,
For only heaven knows!
I like to see my serviettes,
Like flags hung in a line,
And always hang his face towels,
With his hankies next to mine.

It really is quite stupid,
Why I like them so arrayed,
There is no sense or logic
In my actions I'm afraid.
I know if my silk nightie,
Which is feminine and sweet,
Is hung up in the correct way,
It will really look a treat.

So as with satisfaction,
I still find my washing pleasing,
I won't ask him to hang it out,
That's of course, unless it's freezing!

DECISIONS

Decisions are the moments,
When we've taken our Lord's hand,
Because of our life' s destiny,
That He' s already planned.

Don't get upset and wonder,
If your verdict's right or wrong,
Because God knows the future and
The answers all along.

He waits for us to ask Him,
For His guidance on life's way,
He's quick to reassure us,
The moment that we pray.

So if you feel uncertain
What to do, you soon will find,
That letting God decide for you,
Will soon make up your mind.

FASHION SENSE

A funny thing is fashion,
The latest female fad,
I'm puzzled why I find that
It often looks so bad.

Perhaps it is the wearer,
Who bows to man's decree,
Who hasn't got the figure,
The height, the shape or knee,

To sport these shapeless garments,
So drab or loud or bright?
They often seem on females,
Too long, too short, or tight.

Of course in our old photos,
Old-fashioned, out of date,
We also wore those outfits,
That our mums used to hate.

So maybe with some tolerance,
I'll view clothes with new eyes,
And choose a dress that's modern,
Both chic in mode and size.

I'm feeling quite excited,
I'll try this waistless dress,
But in the mirror I see,
I look a frightful mess.

Now what is this that's hanging
Upon the bargain rail?
Oh such a simple, black dress,
How great it's in the sale!

I cannot wait to try it,
It suits me to a tee,
It's not a way-out fashion,
But is exactly me.

So casting padded shoulders,
Bright minis all aside,
I know what feels and looks right,
Is how I should decide.

It's like the style I'm wearing,
It never will outdate,
For me to keep in fashion,
I'm afraid it is too late!

FRIENDSHIP

The loving kindness of a friend,
A hand that's there to take,
Encouragement locked in a smile,
Efforts made for your sake.

A bright greeting, a helpful chore,
The shopping fetched from town,
An invitation out to tea,
Support when you sit down.

The offer of a little ride,
When pains have come and gone,
Are all the things that tired old age,
Needs and depends upon.

Without them suffering and aches,
Sadness turn into tears,
But when a friend is close at hand,
They quickly disperse fears.

Pain can be bad and loneliness,
But with a dear, kind friend,
Their prayers and words are
  comforting,
True friendship's a God-send.

DOES HE REALLY UNDERSTAND?

He looks so cute and charming,
As he hangs his head and pouts,
The innocence surrounding him,
Fills concerned adults with doubts.

"Of course, he's only little,
Do you think he understands?"
Are comments heard as his defiance,
Gets a smack from mother's hands.

"Poor little chap!" - He's screaming!
How his mum regrets her act,
She's wishing that she'd handled him,
With more kindness and with tact.

"Leave it alone, don't touch it!
Oh, you've got it. Well alright."
The toddler knows from this relapse,
It's the way to win the fight.

Just once he's been the victor,
He's persisted, must be right,
It might not be so bad for him,
Though his mum gave him a fright.

He knows now that the next time,
He cries hard when she says "No,"
That she'll give in - she's sighing now,
It's the time to have a go.

She definitely is weakening,
For she sounds fed-up and tired,
So giving a gigantic howl,
He has got what he desired!

UNCONDITIONAL LOVE

There's a love beyond being,
A love beyond hope,
A love that's so strong that
With problems we'll cope.

There's a love beyond reason,
A love beyond thought,
A love which curbs anger,
Prevents a retort.

There's a love full of patience,
A love full of calm,
A love which protects us,
And keeps us from harm.

There's a love for all seasons,
Whatever the weather,
A love which unites us,
And keeps us together.

There's a love in our hearts and
A love in our soul,
A love that can heal us,
Which makes us feel whole.

For as God is within us,
We know He is love,
Let love spread around on
The wings of a dove.

Let our love show its light as
This love is unfurled,
By living this love there'll
Be love in the world.

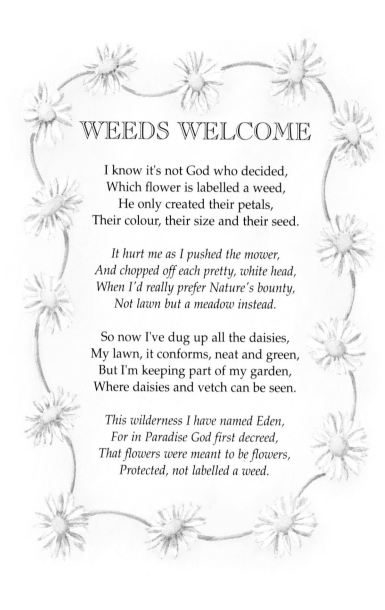

WEEDS WELCOME

I know it's not God who decided,
Which flower is labelled a weed,
He only created their petals,
Their colour, their size and their seed.

It hurt me as I pushed the mower,
And chopped off each pretty, white head,
When I'd really prefer Nature's bounty,
Not lawn but a meadow instead.

So now I've dug up all the daisies,
My lawn, it conforms, neat and green,
But I'm keeping part of my garden,
Where daisies and vetch can be seen.

This wilderness I have named Eden,
For in Paradise God first decreed,
That flowers were meant to be flowers,
Protected, not labelled a weed.

A CERTAIN CURE

I always arrive early,
Making sure I am not late,
And yet I know as always,
I am going to have to wait.
As the waiting room is silent,
A loud cough sounds like a roar,
As pale, unsmiling sufferers,
File sadly through the door.

I know until a mother
With a little child in tow
Arrives, this awful tension
And uneasiness won't go.
As old magazines are sorted
By each patient's nervous hands,
I hope when I'm explaining,
The doctor understands.

My aches have been so dreadful,
All my symptoms so severe,
But when I'm with the doctor,
They will always disappear.
Oh how good, here comes a toddler,
Runny nose, red bobble hat,
He'll soon get patients talking
Discussing this or that.

Now that the quiet is broken,
All the whispering has to end,
I always feel much better
When nattering with a friend.
Overdue is my appointment,
He's not back yet from his calls,
The toddler's cries now shattering
The peace, as down he falls.

That man's cold must be spreading,
If I wasn't ill before,
I've surely caught the 'flu now
Oh, my doctor's at the door!
It's my name he's calling loudly,
- How I wish I'd been to the loo
I can't think what to tell him,
The doctor's wondering too.

"I hope you're feeling better,"
So I say, "I'm pretty well."
- Not really I've felt awful
Soon the truth I'll have to tell.
"Doctor you had better write me
A prescription as before,
Because I've felt much better,
Since I came through the door."

My symptoms sound so trivial,
I am feeling such a fraud,
It's difficult describing,
What needs to be explored.
He does his best to help me,
But I'm struggling to explain,
For it won't be till I've left him
That I'll feel so ill again!

TREASURE

Parents are special,
So guard them with care,
Cherish and love them,
Whilst they are still there.

Cheer them and comfort
Their pains and their fears,
Help them and show them,
Your thanks through the years.

Give them your patience
Now as they grow old,
For the love you have shared is
More precious than gold.

FACE FAMILIAR

I have a certain problem,
That I still have yet to solve,
It's causing a dilemma,
Which somehow I must resolve.

When I am in the country,
Or out walking in the street,
There always is a person,
Quite familiar I shall meet.

I know somewhere I've met her,
By her features and her hair,
Her name I can't remember,
When we met, or why or where.

She says it's nice to see me,
As it's years since we first met,
Now that's a help, but heavens!
Who she is I quite forget.

I didn't have the courage
Then to ask what was her name,
She thinks now that I know it,
And I feel that I'm to blame.

The last time was so awkward,
For on clues her name depends,
And now I'm too embarrassed
To ask her - we're such good friends!

THE ROSE

It shone brightly in my winter garden,
Stood bravely as gales tossed its head,
And it glowed, pouring out its clear message,
As it bloomed in its drab flower bed.

Look, I can survive, so hold on now,
For everything's possible it seems,
You must never give up, keep on fighting,
For your health, for your life, for your dreams.

So I smiled on those wet, dreary mornings,
Cheered up as the dark night's closed in,
For now wrapped in God's love and protection,
My brave rose nor myself would give in.

Now winter is passing it's still there,
Like me a bit care-worn and tired,
But the red rose's love is a symbol,
Of the courage that it has inspired.

Soon I know that my rose will need pruning,
Like me it needs rest and much care,
But ahead spring's new rebirth is stirring,
Which my rose and myself both will share.

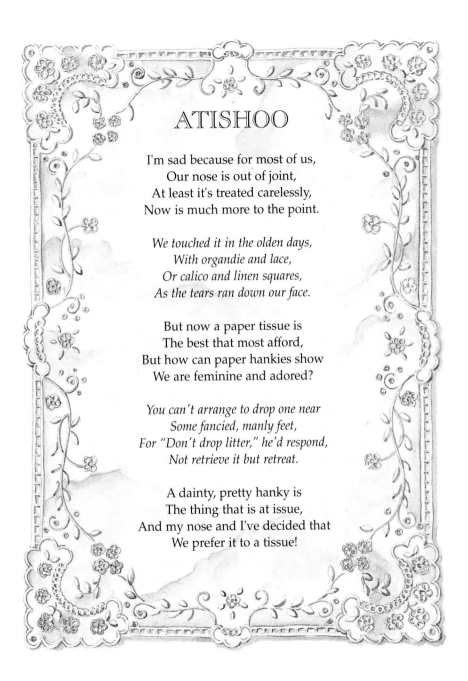

ATISHOO

I'm sad because for most of us,
Our nose is out of joint,
At least it's treated carelessly,
Now is much more to the point.

We touched it in the olden days,
With organdie and lace,
Or calico and linen squares,
As the tears ran down our face.

But now a paper tissue is
The best that most afford,
But how can paper hankies show
We are feminine and adored?

You can't arrange to drop one near
Some fancied, manly feet,
For "Don't drop litter," he'd respond,
Not retrieve it but retreat.

A dainty, pretty hanky is
The thing that is at issue,
And my nose and I've decided that
We prefer it to a tissue!

RIGHT THINKING

All negative thoughts
I've decided must go,
I'll try to say 'Yes',
When I want to say 'No.'
I won't say 'I can't,'
But 'I can only try,'
Accept things that happen,
And not keep wondering why.

I'll make time for hobbies,
Which will brighten my day,
And not let my problems,
Affect things that I say,
There are many homeless,
Hungry, sad, filled with pain,
I'm blessed with so much that
I'll not grumble again.

Today will be good,
For I'm filled now with hope,
With God's love inside,
Now I know I can cope,
No moans and no groans,
No more sighing or dread,
I've found it is best,
To be positive instead.

LOVE RECAPTURED

I saw her in the park again,
Such sweetness in her bearing,
I loved the swan's curve of her neck,
The dress that she was wearing.

She met me shyly with blue eyes,
Which lit up as she saw me,
She knew I was an artist as
She asked, "Please will you draw me?"

My heart was full of tenderness,
I knew I'd always love her,
My fingers touched her shining hair,
My sketch-book poised above her.

She laughed then when I stole a kiss,
And said I was all sticky,
At sixty sketching my grand-child,
I found was rather tricky!

THE TRIBUNAL

They sat and talked, a band of men,
Discussing, asking, why and when,
Was this the moment, age, the time,
When love could defeat greed
  and crime?

Their wisdom had been gained
  through years
Of learning lessons, joy and tears;
They'd lived so many times before,
But knew that there was always more

To know, to learn, to use, to share,
Amongst their brothers living there,
But despair bowed their heads
  with grief,
Until new hope gave them relief.

A little child they saw below,
He stood thin clad in ice and snow,
He threw some biscuits to a bird
The Elders hushed to hear his word.

"It's alright little bird," he said,
"My mummy thinks I'm still in bed."
And as the hungry robin ate,
He squatted down beside the plate.

"It isn't much but I love you,"
He shivered for his toes were blue,
"And I have lots and lots of things,
- Though one day I hope I'll
  have wings."

He left his supper in the snow,
Tiptoed indoors, - they watched
  him go,
Then The Tribunal smiled with joy,
New hope came with this little boy.

The time was near, soon threads of love,
Would weave around, below, above,
With loving thoughts, which
  become real,
The sad world from its wounds
  would heal.

The little boy, he dreamt that night,
With wings he flew in sheer delight.
They all agreed they'd start
  their plan,
To rescue earth and rescue man.

SILENCE IS GOLDEN

My loved one's sympathetic,
As a stillness fills the house,
In fact just at the moment,
It's as quiet as a mouse.

The phone I'd like to answer,
But my husband's brief reply,
Has made him smug and smiling,
And I know the reason why.

He's saving on the phone bill,
For he knows that I can't chatter,
It is going to be a few days,
Until I can have a natter.

I can't call out a comment,
He makes up for what I lack,
And now he grins and teases,
As I cannot answer back.

He's sad I have these symptoms,
But I really have no choice,
He's revelled in the silence,
Since the day I lost my voice!

IN THE STILLNESS

In the stillness
Is the darkness of the night;
In the stillness
Is the wonder of God's light;
In the stillness
I feel strength from God above,
And the whole of my being is
Filled with love.

In the stillness
I feel peace and I feel calm;
In the stillness
I'm protected from all harm;
In the stillness
I lose problems, pressure, pain,
For I know that in God,
I am whole again.

GOLDEN MEMORIES

The day was bright,
Leaves full of light,
Birds singing joyfully,
Midst dappled trees,
Blown by the breeze,
Clouds scudded hastily.
A pigeon cooed,
Woodpecker rude,
Rent silence like a knife,
The heady smell of woodland fell
On senses stirred with life.

Each mossy mound,
Soft scampering sound,
Alerted my keen ears,
When there I saw,
What the tree wore,
My eyes swam soft with tears.
Sweet words were there,
Hand-carved with care,
Upon that old oak tree,
'Here my Jean stood,
She loved this wood,
And most of all loved me.'

I pictured how,
He'd stand there now,
Alone and full of pain,
And see her there,
Wind in her hair,
Dew-faced with gentle rain.
Each tree she'd known,
Clock seeds she'd blown,
The mossy mounds she'd stroked,
The butterflies,
Rooks raucous cries,
Her memory provoked.

How he had laughed,
He'd said "How daft!"
Standing where bluebells grew-,
When Jean had said,
"Let it be read,
I loved these woods and you."
For she had said,
When they were wed,
"We'll leave our mark one day,"
And now I knew,
Each word was true,
For she had had her way.

Although she's gone,
His Jean lives on,
In every woodland walk,
And old Tom feels,
That as time heals,
About her he will talk.
So when he's strong,
We'll go along,
And find once more their tree,
And read again,
The words for then,
From heartbreak he'll be free.

I turned and went,
The day was spent,
The moon cast silver beams,
It filled the night,
With mystic light,
Of memories and dreams.

MY HANDYMAN

It drives me mad, it's got so bad,
I have to plug my ears,
The bathroom tap's still dripping,
I am very close to tears.

As moans abate, my 'Plumber's Mate,'
Turns water off and sings,
He hammers, grumbles, mutters,
As he does mysterious things.

Triumphantly he grins at me,
"The problem's solved," he said,
But now at night I'm hearing,
Sounds of dripping that I dread.

The washer's new, we have no clue,
There are no more solutions,
For now he's turned the tap so tight,
That I can't do my ablutions!

THE POWER OF LOVE

Oh how easy to love,
All that's pretty and good,
The ones who behave, who are kind,
But what do you feel,
When the wicked man smiles,
And atrocities come into mind?

And how easy to love
The red squirrel who's scarce,
How hard to love squirrels when grey,
Why should we decide
Who's deserving our love,
To feed some, yet send others away?

Though we know those in need,
Truly merit our aid,
God made us all just as we are,
And as we are part
Of His great family,
There aren't barriers and no
  colour bar.

It is right to discern
Between good and the bad,
But never judge animal or man,
We all have our faults
And whatever we feel,
We should spread love as far as we can.

To the ugly, the nuisance,
Let us send out God's light,
Find tolerance, forgiveness today,
For only He knows,
Just how much we achieve,
When we touch them with love
  as we pray.

PREPARATION

'I've only got today,' I thought,
Panic rising in my face,
The garden path has lots of weeds,
The hall carpet's a disgrace.'

I rushed and cleaned the living room,
Till at last there was no dust,
I polished, scrubbed and vacuumed,
Then I didn't feel so fussed.

I mopped the sweat which drenched my brow,
As I quickly drank some tea,
I weeded, mowed, then trimmed the hedge,
Satisfied but weary me.

I put away the cleaning things,
And the lawn-mower and the rake,
But when I saw the calendar,
Then I realised my mistake.

I'd turned two pages over - Help!
It is June and not July,
I have another month to go,
Oh, I think I'm going to cry!

For in four weeks I know I'll do
Still the same, I'll clean and fuss,
I'll rush and slave, get in a flap,
Just because you're visiting us!

A HOUSEWIFE'S FATE

The morning that I've overslept,
My curtains are still drawn,
And haven't placed the cushion where
The chair is frayed and worn;

When breakfast dishes are not washed,
My hair is in a mess,
That's when the visitors arrive,
Unexpected, you can guess.

But now I've polished, vac'd and cleaned,
My windows sparkle bright,
I've placed the flowers more tastefully,
No speck of dust in sight;

Lonely I sit, in spotless state,
Thinking how pleased I'd be,
If at this moment visitors,
Would decide to visit me!

MARY'S VISIT

It was on Easter Monday,
That Mary passed my way,
Sun-sparkling was the weather,
And spring-filled was the day.
I hadn't heard her coming,
Of her presence unaware,
I stopped what I was doing,
And simply found her there.

A little white-haired lady,
Whose smile was sweet and kind,
-A photo of my Grandma,
At once came into mind.
I gave a friendly greeting,
And then she said to me,
"How nice of you to stop work,
To talk so readily."

She told me she was lonely,
-How could she not be glad,
When all around was beauty?
She mustn't feel so sad.
A sudden impulse took me,
I said "Let's have some tea,
Enjoy the scent of mown grass,
And spend some time with me."

Although it was the first time,
That we had met that day,
Somehow I felt I knew her,
Had met her on life's way.
Her pleasure was so touching,
Sipping her tea with me,
Observing birds, the flowers,
An early bumble bee.

Wrapped in a rug to warm her,
She gave a happy smile,
"It's such a treat to sit here,
And chat a little while.
I'm on my own, so lonely,
And in this sunny weather,
I couldn't bear my longing,
When seeing folks together."

I kissed her, as she thanked me,
Turned, waved a last goodbye,
But she had disappeared,
Just lane, hedges and sky!
I haven't seen her since then,
A mystery she'll remain,
Unless perhaps at Easter,
I shall see her once again?

WHO COULD ASK FOR MORE?

A blessing came this summer,
A darling little boy,
As flowers bloomed bright to welcome him,
He brought both love and joy.

He came to them so bonny,
Dark-haired, though he'll be fair,
They counted all his little toes,
So perfect lying there.

How sleepy and how cuddly,
So tiny, compact, neat,
They laughed because their little one,
Has such enormous feet.

As mother holds him closely,
And love stirs in her heart,
She knows that with their baby son,
A whole new life will start.

She is so glad her husband,
Is patient, kind and strong,
With his protection and support,
She knows things won't go wrong.

Their hearts are full to bursting,
With loving care and pride,
Although they both watched anxiously,
Each moment that he cried.

They've called their baby Oliver,
This child that they adore,
But they have vowed their little son,
Need never ask for more!

THE SAME DIFFERENCE

"They are different," you said,
"They are nothing like us,
For their creed and their faith's not the same."
But the truth is, I know,
That if we all love God,
There is no need to give love a name.

If we're rich, or we're poor,
If we label ourselves,
Middle class, upper class or some such,
When we take off our clothes,
Or we kneel down in prayer,
Any difference you'll see isn't much.

For we're all sons of God,
And we know God is love,
We're related, our name is the same,
So whatever religion,
No label I need,
For we play the identical game.

As our 'Father' is God,
He's your father and mine,
Then our love doesn't need name or place,
For we are but a spark,
Of God's love so divine,
One religion, one colour, one race.

ONE TOO MANY

I've had a glass of sherry,
It's gone straight to my head,
For rarely do I have a drink,
Except when folks are wed.

My head feels light and fuzzy,
I'm giggling down the phone,
I know he's disapproving by
The vicar's troubled tone.

My sherry was a present,
Next time I'll have a biscuit,
For on an empty stomach now,
I never more shall risk it.

It's made me flushed and sleepy,
Though strangely quite elated,
It seems that on one sherry I'm
Completely inebriated!

THE CAROL SINGERS

Each cherub face was flushed with cold,
Young voices sweet and shrill,
Sang of the story angels told,
To shepherds on the hill.

Deep in their pockets hands were thrust,
Cheeks rosy, shiny-eyed,
Their carols full and clear they sang,
Off key, although they tried.

They weren't the usual urchin types,
Rude youths or giggling pair,
They smiled a sweet yet earnest smile,
And innocence was there.

Politely then they said their thanks,
In these days such a treat,
Then as they stood, like crystal stars
Snow sparkled in the street.

It sprinkled on their hair, their nose,
And settled on their coats,
They grinned brimful of Christmas fun,
Glee chuckling in their throats.

Carols and snow, how right it seemed,
As we both stood enraptured;
We smiled because for just a while,
Christmas magic we had captured.

HOLD ON TO JOY

In my hand I held you,
A moment ago,
Where are you? I found you,
And I loved you so.
You filled me with gladness,
You brightened my day,
Dear joy that was mine,
Why did you slip away?

My mind was so peaceful,
I felt such relief,
For I was now tranquil,
Had lost jagged grief.
I felt so elated I'd found you again,
Intended from now on,
That I'd feel no more pain.

And then in a moment,
You left as I sighed,
You hid, disappeared,
As in torment I cried;
I ask now, please joy,
You'll quickly return,
It's you that I long for,
It is you that I yearn.

What's this? There's a flicker
Of hope in my heart,
An expectant promise,
That soon joy will start
To tiptoe, then shine
In my troubled soul,
Oh joy, you're so welcome,
I will now become whole.

The healing has started,
I've held on to you,
I've caught you and wrapped you,
Around all I do;
A spark you are now,
A flame soon you'll be,
Oh, thank you dear joy,
For returning to me.

DIET DILEMMA

There are diets by the dozen,
To aid us with our size,
There's walking and there's jogging,
For the healthy and the wise.

Now aerobics, isometrics,
Squash, yoga, keep fit hours,
And every kind of treatment,
Are dictated by high powers.

So we read, digest, determine,
Which path that we should take,
How fervent are the efforts,
In those first few days we make.

But our scales remain reluctant,
We don't get very far,
So we decide that fate decreed,
That we stay the way we are!

COMMON SENSES

I saw God in a flower today,
I saw God in the trees;
I saw Him in the butterflies,
The busy, humming bees.

I felt God in a loving hand,
I felt God in the sun;
I felt Him in my cosy home,
In warmth, in love, in fun.

I heard God in the whispering wind,
I heard God in song birds;
I heard Him in the way you spoke,
In loving, kindly words.

God's perfume filled the air today,
In fresh mown grass and sea;
In damp, moist earth after the rain,
In shrubs and lilac tree.

I tasted water from a spring,
Fresh honey from the bee;
With my five senses I thank God,
For giving them to me.

RELEASE

As I let go the tension,
The worries, doubts and fears,
I feel the anxious trembling,
Dissolving with my tears.

I am relieved and tranquil,
As God takes me in hand,
And all my trials and testings,
I now can understand.

I see them as a challenge,
Accept now what they meant,
I know that they were lessons,
And that's why they were sent.

I face them now with courage,
At least I really try,
And ask no more the questions,
What for? How long? Or why?

For now these times are over,
As joy and peace return,
I have been made much stronger,
By things I've had to learn.

Acceptance is my key word,
For God is by my side,
His presence gave me courage,
And love my tears has dried.

THE DEERSTALKER HAT

"Look at me!" he said,
Pointing to his head,
His flat feet splayed out with pride.
"How d'you like my hat,
What d'you think of that?"
I felt laughter rise inside.

But I had to stare,
Though to be quite fair,
Very chic and smart was he,
For with tied-up flaps,
It beat all the caps,
And polite I had to be.

For perched smart and trim,
On the top of him,
Sherlock Holmes he would have shamed,
For no normal gear,
Did he display here,
As much higher his fashions aimed.

But the bow on top!
Tears I couldn't stop,
Laughter spluttered down my cheeks,
Then quickly replaced,
I admired his taste,
Or we'd not have spoken for weeks!

THE ROBIN

It was still dark as night,
And the morning seemed dreary,
When suddenly sounded,
A voice, sweet and cheery,
As it brightened the day,
It too lightened my heart,
It was so full of hope,
Gave my day a new start.

It was such a small thing,
Which gave life a new meaning,
Which came from the branch,
On my window-sill leaning,
As I listened, I thrilled,
To its beautiful voice,
For it sounded so glad,
It made my heart rejoice.

Though the cold and wet winter
Had left everywhere dripping,
Its song of delight,
Came stirring and tripping;
As it challenged the storms
And moments of strife,
It was joined by the rooks
And shrill cries of sea life.

And as loud gulls replied,
With their shrieking and calling,
Soft snow-flakes like feathers,
Came drifting and falling,
But now nothing I felt,
In this day could go wrong,
As I listened and thrilled,
To its heart-warming song.

Then my robin flew off,
It's wings darting and whirring,
And hope deep within me,
Was waking and stirring,
Now no longer distressed,
At not sleeping at five,
Its brave message I heard,
"Thank you God, I'm alive!"

WELCOME AUTUMN

The swans now arrive,
And the air is alive,
With the whirring and stirring of wings,
As moorland now glints,
With bright autumnal tints,
My heart moves with the beauty of things.

Wild waves roar and tumble,
As winds whip and rumble,
Whirling rainbow leaves down
*   on the grass,*
The crane-fly's frustration,
Is turned to elation,
As it's freed from a web as I pass.

Ripe apples now drop,
Give a bountiful crop,
Luscious grass, emerald green
   from the rain,
As the summer now ends,
Just like greeting old friends,
Autumn days bring me
   pleasure again.

Red rose-hips enhancing,
Lace cobwebs entrancing,
Mellow days bringing warmth
*   and blue skies,*
Now as God rearranges,
The seasonal changes,
Every day I find full of surprise.

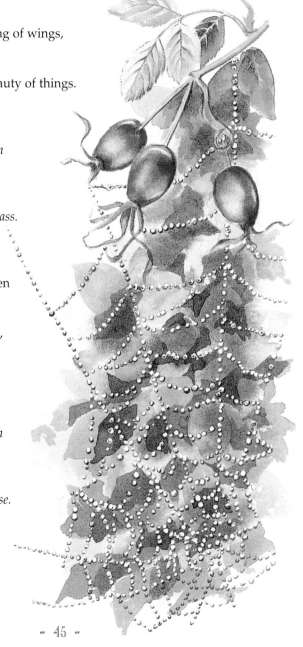

TEENAGERS

They're clumsy, they're untidy,
They annoy us, stay out late;
They surprise us with their thoughtfulness,
Are considerate, are great.

They're emotional and touchy,
Frequently they're awkward, rude;
But they often show maturity,
If I'm in a funny mood.

Their loud music drives us crazy,
And their fashions - what a mess!
Yet they're such a source of laughter and
Full of fun and happiness.

We wouldn't be without them
'Wish they'd get that car to start!'
But the day my fledglings leave the nest,
I just know I'll break my heart!

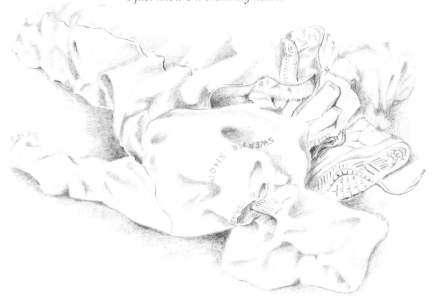

REVIVAL

I've awoken again,
I'm alive and I'm free
Of the sadness, the hurt
That has surrounded me.
It is slipping away
Now as soft as the night,
And ahead of me I
Can see sunshine and light.

For my soul is at peace
And my angels agree,
That I leave grief behind,
And I find the real me,
They now gently unfold,
Their great, warm, healing wings,
And they point the way forward
To most, wonderful things.

There's a stirring inside,
As my restlessness goes,
There's a feeling of strength,
Of that something one knows;
There's a lightness of step
And a joy in my heart,
For I know God still waits
For my life's work to start.

As I gaze at the stars,
At the flowers and the trees,
New excitement and love's
Carried fresh on the breeze,
I'm recovering at last
From my grief and my pain,
Oh I thank you Dear God,
That I'm living again!

GOLDEN MENACE

My husband has got an obsession,
As he spies one his face goes quite red,
At the thought of mass multiplication,
Things suddenly come to a head.

He rushes off to his diversion,
His lone target full blown, in its prime,
As he plucks the offending creation,
I laugh at the innocent crime.

For Nature invented a method,
To increase and extend its own stock;
Now what does he regard with such passion?
The delicate, dandelion clock!

THE WAYS OF A SMILE

Smile today and every day,
Although your heart is breaking,
Smile when tears are close to you,
And when your heart is aching;
Smile when you are feeling down,
And all around feels rotten,
Smile and your depression will,
Soon pass and be forgotten.

Moan and you will find a moan,
Will return as an answer,
Moan and you will soon find out,
It's spreading like a cancer;
Moan when you are feeling ill,
You'll find you feel no better,
Moans will never set you free,
They chain, restrict and fetter.

Smile at strangers as you pass,
You'll find a smile returning,
Smile at one whose glance is black,
It's just the thing they're yearning,
Smile although you've had enough,
A day both hard and trying,
Smile in spite of all these things,
You'll find your troubles dying.

Snap at people whom you meet,
You'll find their words are biting,
Snap and say rash, hasty words,
You'll soon have loved ones fighting;
Snap and show impatience now,
And soon you will be lonely,
Stop, it soon can be controlled
By you, but by you only.

Soon you'll find surrounding you,
People are calm and cheerful,
Confident that they can come
For comfort when they're tearful,
You will find your life enriched,
By gladness and not sorrow,
So now you can look forward to,
A hopeful, bright tomorrow.

SPIRITUAL PATHWAY

It is not where I think I am going,
It is not any heights I've achieved,
But the part that in life I am playing,
And the spiritual strength I've received.

It is now, not the future's important,
It is how I face problems and fears,
It's the challenging tests I am passing,
As God's light and His hope dry my tears.

I am where I should be at this moment,
And the thoughts that I think I need now,
My emotions and feelings are lessons,
I won't ask where I'm going or how.

It's acceptance of knowing a loved one,
Is still living and happy and real,
And believing my time on this earth plane's,
But a spoke in the evolutionary wheel.

God's divine spark I know is within me,
To be nearer then God couldn't be,
The potential of His love and power,
Is right there in the true, perfect me.

So each day I shall learn how to use it,
My divine spark ignite, make it shine,
And in seeking the truth, I shall find it,
For in God's light I'll also find mine.

THE DRESS FITTING

My daughter's getting married,
My mind is in a whirl,
It doesn't seem five minutes
Since she was a little girl.

She's dressed in gleaming satin,
A dream of pearls and lace,
Transformed into a princess,
Flushed excitement on her face.

What happened to my baby,
The toddler, then the child,
That moody, awkward youngster,
My teenager, sweet and wild?

This elegant young woman
Can life still be the same?
Her love's gone to another,
And she's changing home and name.

So grown up and so lovely.
I feel I've lost her now,
But I must not be selfish,
I'll accept, I'll cope somehow.

But what's this in the mirror?
I see she's near to tears,
I'll put my arms around her,
Why! She's full of doubts and fears.

At last I've reassured her,
And smiling at each other,
I know my daughter will not change,
I'll always be her mother.

NOT HIS DAY

He said he'd do the shopping,
As I had so much to do,
We'd been away for ages,
And my chores were overdue.

I unpacked and I tidied,
Sorted laundry into piles,
I did a lot of washing,
Satisfied was full of smiles.

I sat to have a breather,
Drinking thankfully my tea,
When Hubby returned fuming,
Very upset I could see.

He'd done a lot of buying,
Then he'd queued to check them out,
But some things he'd forgotten,
And he couldn't turn about.

So crowded and frustrated,
Pressured, fussed, fed-up and rushed,
His packing into boxes,
Caused some items to be crushed;

Then he withdrew his wallet,
Found as he prepared to pay,
He had more goods than money,
Oh, it wasn't quite his day!

Discarding certain packets,
He dashed swiftly to the car,
Came home, then soothed by coffee,
He'd return, it wasn't far.

But as he called out crossly,
"I'll be glad when this day passes,"
My heart sank as he shouted,
"Oh help no! I've lost my glasses!"

TO SHARE IS TO CARE

Health is all the wealth we need,
A richness we can share,
With others not so fortunate,
Who need our love and care.

A friendly word, a welcome smile,
A sign we understand,
A loving hug, a gentle strength,
A sincere caring hand.

It's all the efforts that we make,
A sacrifice, a gift,
A contribution, sale of work,
Which can give life a lift

To those who're suffering each day,
And need a helping hand,
Whose lives depend on folk like us,
Who care and understand.

So as we now attempt to help,
All those who live in pain,
Remember that our efforts can
Change tears to smiles again.

WHAT WILL THE DOCTOR THINK?

Have you ever noticed that
The moment you're in bed,
Decided that you will give in,
Pains in your back and head,
That as you look around the room,
It all seems so untidy,
And how you wish your
  'bedroom day,'
Was Monday and not Friday?

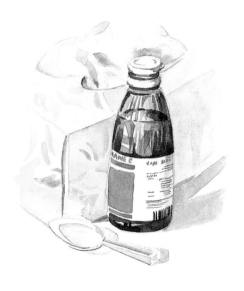

*As watery-eyed you see some dust
Upon your dressing table,
You'd love to fetch the duster now
If only you were able.
Some smudgy marks upon the door,
His shoes thrown in disorder,
Oh, I would love a daily help,
If I could but afford her!*

My beauty aids are disarrayed,
Bed-cover in a heap,
Oh how can I recover when
I'll never go to sleep?
My cheery, helpful husband brings
In medicines and drinks,
And he is not at all concerned
At what the doctor thinks.

*But when he's safely reading his
Newspaper in the chair,
I'll drag myself around the room,
And tidy here and there.
Ah, that's a little better now,
At least the bed looks neat,
No longer trailing bed-sheets lie
All creased around my feet.*

If Hubby caught me in the act,
His patience would decrease,
And though I'm feeling terrible,
At least I'll rest in peace.
He really hasn't noticed yet
A difference at all,
So I can snuggle down until
The doctor comes to call!

TOMORROW NEVER COMES

Tell people today that you love them,
Or one day it could be too late,
Don't ever hold back something thoughtful,
Or decide that a kind deed can wait.

A moment of loving can vanish,
Awareness of grief disappear,
Show now how you feel for your dear ones,
Then you'll magic a smile from a tear.

Don't let in your life come a moment,
When things in your heart are still stored,
And ones whom you love have departed,
Still not knowing that they were adored.

Today is the moment to say them,
Those words which are tricky to find,
You'll have no regrets only gladness,
That you said them if you're left behind.

RICHNESS

Richness for the greedy is
The money they can hoard,
Richness for the homeless is
A place they can afford;
Richness to the debutante
Is finery, fast cars,
Richness to an astrologer,
Is the glory of the stars.

Richness is the quality
Of life, the way we live,
Richness isn't what we keep,
But what we all can give;
Richness is the joyfulness,
Of children when they play,
Richness is the tint of trees,
On a sunny Autumn day.

Richness is the friends we have,
The love that we receive,
Richness is in music, art,
The truth that we believe,
Richness is good health, not wealth,
So make the most of it,
Richness is kindness received,
By the ones who're not so fit.

Richness to the lonely is
A visit from a friend,
Richness to the starving is
Food supplies that never end,
Richness to the suffering,
Is a sympathetic ear,
Richness is a tender hug,
And a smile which brings you cheer.

Richness in our inner selves,
Is what we can find here,
Seeking God in quietness,
Helps problems disappear.
When there is peace, tranquility,
Decisions can be made,
And in the stillness, strength is given
To face testings unafraid.

For filling thoughts with love and light,
Unite us with our brother,
And all the richness that we need,
We'll find in one another

THE SALE

We made a special effort,
Were early out of bed
We ate our breakfast hurriedly,
Newspapers still unread.

We left milk on the doorstep,
Then rain began to pour;
Jumped in the car - then back again,
We hadn't locked the door!

The journey was horrific,
Each traffic light turned red,
The thought that we'd be just too late,
Kept running through my head.

Each time that we were held up,
I bowed my head and prayed,
And hoped that they would have one left,
Although we were delayed.

At last we did arrive there,
Our timing really fine,
The store opened in half an hour,
We'd thought it was at nine.

Triumphantly we entered,
And found our 'Bargain' there,
We placed it on the counter top,
A joyful, happy pair.

So pleased we could afford it,
No need to save or borrow,
But what a shock as we went to pay,
The sale begins tomorrow!

MY PERFECT DAY

Now for a perfect day, I thought,
As I jumped out of bed,
Keen plans for chores and little tasks,
Were spinning through my head.
I washed and dressed, I made some tea,
And sipped it with delight,
The sun shone down from soft, blue skies,
The day was clear and bright.

Fine weather drew me out of doors,
I thought, I'll mow the lawn,
But first I'll trim the roses - Ouch,
That hurt, that wretched thorn!
With plastered thumb, the mower on,
I sniffed grass-perfumed air,
When suddenly the mower stopped
Could I do a repair?

I unplugged and retested it,
All tried it would not go,
Oh, well, I'll put the washer on,
Instead of trying to mow.
The washing turning merrily,
I thought I'll take a bite,
I burned the toast, then broke my nail,
My thoughts were hardly white.

The washing's still, I'll take it out,
I opened up the door,
With frantic hands I tried to stop
The flood upon the floor.
I yelled as I saw what I'd done,
My thoughts I can't confess,
With buckets, bowls and mopping cloths,
I cleared up all the mess.

I sank exhausted to the floor,
And stared in sheer dismay,
Oh what was happening to this,
My bright and cheerful day?
I grabbed the clothes and hung them
Engrossed in thoughts of wrath,
I didn't see the garden hose,
There lying on the path.

I knocked my knee as I fell down,
What words I didn't say,
There couldn't be another thing,
Or I'd be turning grey!
I went inside and nursed my leg,
Then bandaged, tried to think,
I'll vacuum first, the lounge and hall
Then I'll feel in the pink.

The cleaner sucked and then it blew,
Then groaning fizzled out,
I stamped my foot, threw up my hands,
What was this all about?
This can't go on, it's not my day,
I'll visit my best friend
The answer phone - she's out of course,
This really is the end!

Well I give up! I'll do no more,
I'll have a nice sit down,
A coffee and my library book,
Will take away my frown.
I sigh content, a quiet read
Will stop me feeling blue,
Oh, no, what's this?
My library book
Is five days overdue!

BLUEBELLS

Their beauty took our breath away,
A sea of blue, this day in May,
In woods and valleys, carpets spread,
Where deer and fox and rabbit tread.

Their nodding heads join stars of light,
Wild garlic scattered, virgin white,
Red campions cannot compete,
With bluebells lying round our feet.

In verdant fields, upon the banks,
Beneath the trees, they stand in ranks,
Their hue outshines the parsley's mass
Of garland heads above the grass.

Hawthorn is bursting into bloom,
But bluebell beauty has no room
For other flowers.
Their sweet array,
Enchant us all, this day in May.

PEACEFULNESS

Peace is walking down a lane,
Dry earth refreshed by gentle rain,
It's glimpsing glowing stars at night,
And found in silent seabirds flight.

It's there when moonlight casts its beams,
To warm our hearts and fill our dreams,
It's with the gentle, lapping tide,
Or dozing by the fireside.

It's found when Springtime gardens fill
With blossom and bright daffodil,
It's everywhere if you just look,
In music, art and well-loved book.

Open your eyes and you will find,
Beauty of sight and heart and mind,
For trees and moors, green hills and dales,
Are where God's harmony prevails.

And though man's world has much unrest,
It's up to us to stay unstressed,
There are a thousand ways to find,
Contentment, joy and peace of mind.

WALK WITH ANGELS

Walk with angels, tread with God,
Your sleep as light as a feather,
With joy and love to keep you warm,
You'll face life's stormy weather.

Hold out your hands, reach out for light,
Each link will make you strong,
Now feel God's cloak as it protects,
And you will do no wrong.

As angels sweep your guilt away,
At failure and distress,
Their love will guard and comfort you,
Fill you with happiness.

So be aware of angels who
Will guide you day by day,
And know that you are not alone,
They're just a thought away.

So turn to them, reach out to them,
They'll not desert you - never.
What comfort now as hand in hand,
With them you'll walk forever.

GOD'S PROTECTION

At the start of the day,
Meditate or just pray,
And then nothing can
   unrest provoke;
As you surround yourself,
With the pure light of God,
It's a beautiful,
Protective cloak.

For this cloak is made up
Of such wonderful things,
Of serenity, healing and love;
Though you travel afar,
Know wherever you are,
You'll be safe with
The care from above.

For when fear is released,
And God's love keeps you warm,
No intrusion can disturb your soul,
And as doubtfulness goes,
Self assurance then grows,
As the healing
Of Christ makes you whole.

There will only be light,
As you go on life's way,
It will spring from your
   innermost being,
As you smile in the street,
You'll affect all you meet,
For it's God's light
That they will be seeing.

So as troubles and ills,
Are dispersed by your cloak,
Irritations are swept clean away,
Feeling soothed and restored,
Never angry or bored,
You'll attract love
And light through the day.

So don't ever cast off,
God's most beautiful cloak,
Which is there to be used and is free,
You'll be tranquil and calm,
And protected from harm,
Put it on now
And just wait and see.